I Can Make

SLIPPERY SLIME

by Cody Crane

Rookie STAR™ MakerSpace Projects

SCHOLASTIC

TABLE OF CONTENTS

GLOWING SLIME

GALAXY SLIME

FLUFFY SLIME

ARE YOU A MAKER?

Makers are inventors, artists, and builders. By creating the different slimes in this book, you can be a maker, too! You will learn how to make three types of slippery slime: galaxy slime, fluffy slime, and glowing slime.

These projects look very different from one another. But they are all slime. And they all work using **chemistry**.

You don't need to be a science whiz to make slime, and you don't need fancy tools. Project materials can be found around the house or at a craft store. Are you creative and up for an adventure? Then you've got what it takes. Let's get started!

GALAXY SLIME

GLOWING SLIME

FLUFFY SLIME

BEFORE YOU START...

- Find a clean countertop or table to work on. Cover the area with newspaper.
- Wear old clothes or a smock.
- Wear gloves during each project.
- Clean up when you're finished. Throw slime away in the trash—NOT the sink. Wash your hands after each project.
- *And remember to ask permission before using household products.*

You will need an adult's help with some steps. They will be marked with this warning sign:

YOU CAN MAKE
GALAXY SLIME

A galaxy is a huge group of stars in space. The stars we see from Earth belong to the Milky Way galaxy. The Milky Way contains billions of stars. They circle the galaxy's center. You can make slime that shimmers and swirls just like the Milky Way.

Most things in the world are a solid, a liquid, or a gas. These are the three main types of **matter**. But slime is different. It acts like both a solid and a liquid. You can roll it into a firm ball. But when you stop rolling the slime, it will **ooze** through your fingers.

DISCOVER MORE ABOUT

MATTER

SOLID

LIQUID

GAS

Matter makes up everything around you. The smallest building blocks of matter are **atoms**. The atoms in a solid are tightly packed together. So it keeps its shape.

A liquid's atoms easily slide past one another. So it flows. A gas' atoms move freely. They will spread out to fill a space. Only water can exist in all three states.

8

GALAXY SLIME IS MADE WITH...

FOOD COLORING
is a dye that gives the slime color.

GLITTER
is tiny pieces of plastic. Light reflects off their shiny surfaces. That makes the slime shimmer.

SHAMPOO
is a thick liquid that sticks to particles of cornstarch. That holds the slime together.

CORNSTARCH

comes from a type of sugar found in corn. It makes the slime thick.

9

INSTRUCTIONS

1

Pour the cornstarch into one of the bowls.

2

Carefully sprinkle the glitter on top of the cornstarch.

SAFETY NOTE

⚠ Food coloring can stain. Try not to get it on hands, clothes, or furniture. If you do, wash thoroughly with soapy water right away.

Add the shampoo to the bowl and slowly stir everything together. If the mixture is too dry, add another drop or two of shampoo. If the mixture is too wet, sprinkle in a bit more cornstarch.

Keep stirring until the slime is completely mixed. Then use your hands to knead the slime until smooth.

⚠ Divide the slime evenly among the three bowls. Add a drop of food coloring to each bowl. (Use a different color for each one.) Mix in the food coloring.

SEE IT SHIMMER

Use your hands to roll each colored slime into a tube. Lay the three tubes of slime side by side on a paper plate. Twist and swirl them together. The shiny bits of glitter will catch the light, making the colorful slime sparkle.

TEST IT

Roll the slime into a ball. It holds its shape like a solid. Now let the slime ooze from your hand onto the plate. It should flow like a liquid. You can store your slime in an airtight container.

CHANGE IT

1. Add more glitter to your slime. Does it ooze as easily as before?

2. Make slime with more colors. Add them into your galaxy slime. How do the colors of the slime change as you keep playing with it?

3. Add other things to your slime, like beads, sequins, confetti stars, or tiny foam balls. How does this change the slime's texture?

3. The texture becomes rougher and thicker.

2. The colors blend together over time, forming a different color.

1. No. It's grittier, so it oozes less.

YOU CAN MAKE
FLUFFY SLIME

How slime looks and feels depends on its ingredients. But that is not all. Some slime recipes rely on a **chemical reaction** to work. It causes the substances you mix together to turn into something brand-new. That new thing is stretchy, squishy slime! Whip up some fluffy goop to see for yourself how a chemical reaction works.

Stir together some salt and pepper in a bowl. Do the two items change? No. They are still salt and pepper. But that is not always what happens when you mix things together. Sometimes ingredients react. The original substances break apart or combine to form brand-new things.

DISCOVER MORE ABOUT

POLYMERS

Glue is made up of **polymers**. These particles are big, but they can still slide past each other. That's why glue is thick but runny. Adding certain chemicals to glue causes a chemical reaction that makes the glue's polymers link together. They have a much harder time moving around.

FLUFFY SLIME IS MADE WITH...

FOOD COLORING

is a dye that gives the slime color.

CONTACT LENS SOLUTION

contains a small amount of borax. It causes a chemical reaction with the glue's polymers, making them bind together.

GLUE

contains large particles called polymers. They are made up of long chains of repeating groups of molecules.

SHAVING CREAM

is filled with bubbles, which give the slime a fluffy texture.

15

INSTRUCTIONS

1 Pour the glue into the bowl.

2 Use the spoon or craft stick to scoop the shaving cream into the bowl.

TOOLS

☐ Medium mixing bowl

☐ Plastic spoon or flat wooden craft stick

MATERIALS

☐ One bottle school glue (4 fluid ounces)

☐ 1 cup foaming shaving cream

☐ Food coloring

☐ 4 tablespoons contact lens solution (must list boric acid as an ingredient; see safety note)

SAFETY NOTE

⚠️ Food coloring can stain. And the boric acid present in contact lens solution can be a bit corrosive to the skin. Be sure to wear gloves as you work!

Add a few drops of food coloring to the bowl. Then add the contact lens solution.

Mix the ingredients together. Stir until well combined. (The ingredients need to be mixed well for the project to work.)

Use your hands to knead and stretch the slime. Stretch and squish it until it is no longer sticky. This may take a while.

GIVE IT A SQUISH

Your slime should look smooth and fluffy. If it doesn't, knead the slime some more until it reaches the right consistency. Then give your slime a shake. It should form a wobbly blob.

TEST IT

Squeeze and stretch your slime. What does it feel like? Poke your fingers into the slime. You should hear tiny popping sounds. That's the bubbles in the shaving cream bursting. When you're finished playing with your slime, you can store it in an airtight container.

CHANGE IT

1. Mix more shaving cream into your slime. Does it become fluffier?

2. Let the slime sit overnight. What does it look like now?

3. ⚠ Cover the slime with plastic wrap and place it in the freezer for 15 minutes. Does that make it less wobbly and stretchy?

1. It will become even foamier.
2. Bubbles will have risen to the top and popped, leaving holes in the slime.
3. Yes. It will be stiffer and tougher to pull.

YOU CAN MAKE
GLOWING SLIME

Did you know that your body makes slime? It is the boogers that are inside your nose! You can make slime that seems a lot like snot—just not as gross. This slime also does something that real boogers do not. It glows in the dark.

Glow-in-the-dark objects contain special chemicals that soak up light. Then they slowly give off the energy as a glow. The chemicals eventually run out of energy. Then they stop glowing. But you can put them in a sunny spot to recharge. Then they will glow again.

DISCOVER MORE ABOUT
LIGHT

| Ultraviolet | VISIBLE | Infrared |

The sun gives off a lot of energy as light. The sun's bright light that we see is called visible light. The sun also gives off rays we can't see. Those are ultraviolet (UV) and infrared light. UV light charges up glow-in-the-dark objects, like your slime.

GLOWING SLIME IS MADE WITH...

3-IN-1

is shampoo, conditioner, and body wash together. It has chemicals that help it foam and clean. Salt causes these chemicals to clump together. That forms a gel.

SALT

triggers a chemical reaction. It causes the 3-in-1 to thicken.

GLOW-IN-THE-DARK PAINT

absorbs light. Over time it releases the light energy, which can be seen in the dark.

PROJECT 3

TOOLS

- Small mixing bowl
- Plastic spoon or flat wooden craft stick
- Paper plate

MATERIALS

- ¼ cup 3-in-1 shampoo, conditioner, and body wash
- 1 teaspoon glow-in-the-dark paint
- ½ teaspoon salt

INSTRUCTIONS

1 Measure the 3-in-1 and pour it into the bowl.

2 ⚠️ Measure the paint and add it to the bowl.

SAFETY NOTE

⚠️ Glow-in-the-dark paint can stain. Try not to get it on hands, clothes, or furniture. If you do, wash thoroughly with soapy water right away.

3

Sprinkle the salt on top of the other ingredients in the bowl.

4

Stir the mixture until it begins to look like jelly.

5

Let the slime mixture sit in direct sunlight for one minute.

MAKE IT GLOW

Find a room that can be made dark. The darker the room, the better. Turn off all the lights. Your slime will glow. Don't see anything? Set your slime in the sun for a longer time. Then try again.

TEST IT

Time how long your slime's glow lasts. After a while, it will release all of its stored energy. Then the slime will no longer glow. Set it back in the sun to get more glowing power. Store your slime in an airtight container.

CHANGE IT

1. Place your slime in various dark spots in your home. Find where it glows best.

2. Leave your slime in a dark place overnight. Does it still glow in the morning?

3. Have an adult help you charge your slime under different indoor lights. Try LED, incandescent, and fluorescent lightbulbs. Do any of them cause your slime to glow?

1. The darkest room is best.
2. No. It needs to be recharged.
3. Only fluorescent bulbs give off enough UV light to charge it.

SLIMY CREATURES

You already learned that people make slime. So do a lot of other living things. Slime helps them stay safe, get around, and catch food.

ACH...EWW

The inside of your **nose** is coated in mucus, or snot. This sticky stuff traps germs and dust particles when you breathe. That stops them from reaching your lungs and making you sick.

SLIPPERY FISH

Hagfish are eel-like animals that live in the ocean. When attacked, a hagfish oozes slime from its skin—lots of it. One hagfish can make four cups of slime in less than a second! The slick slime makes the fish hard to grab. That allows it to slip away from danger.

SLUG

SNAIL

SNAIL TRAIL

Snails and **slugs** have a coating of slime on their bellies. It helps them glide more easily as they move. The slime is not just slippery. It is also sticky. The slime allows snails and slugs to climb up surfaces. It keeps them from falling off things like trees and walls.

STICKY SPIT

A chameleon has a really long tongue that can stretch twice the length of the animal's body. The chameleon uses it to catch bugs. The end of this lizard's tongue is covered in slimy spit that sticks to insects. The chameleon can then pull its meal right into its mouth.

CAVE SNOT

Some cave walls drip with slime. Inside the slime are millions of tiny microbes. They are creatures too small to see with the naked eye. The microbes make the slime their home. It keeps them safe.

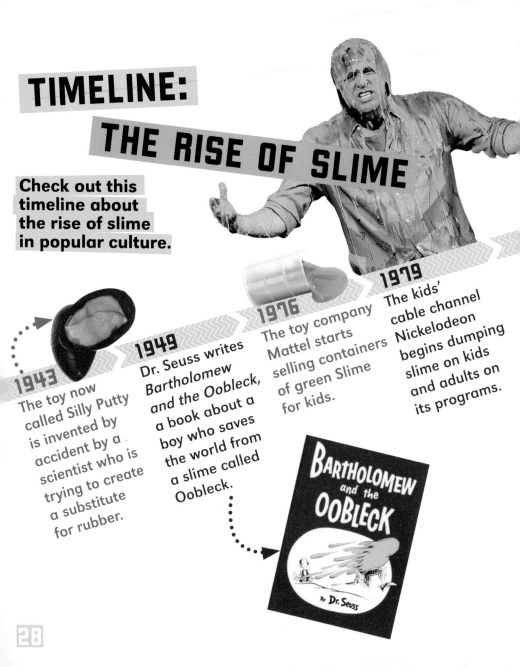

TIMELINE:
THE RISE OF SLIME

Check out this timeline about the rise of slime in popular culture.

1943
The toy now called Silly Putty is invented by accident by a scientist who is trying to create a substitute for rubber.

1949
Dr. Seuss writes Bartholomew and the Oobleck, a book about a boy who saves the world from a slime called Oobleck.

1976
The toy company Mattel starts selling containers of green Slime for kids.

1979
The kids' cable channel Nickelodeon begins dumping slime on kids and adults on its programs.

BARTHOLOMEW and the OOBLECK
By Dr. Seuss

1984
A slime-covered ghost named Slimer is featured in the movie *Ghostbusters*.

1987
In the cartoon series *Teenage Mutant Ninja Turtles*, toxic slime turns ordinary turtles into superheroes.

1992
Mattel releases a goopy toy called Gak based on Nickelodeon's popular slime.

2016
Videos showing makers creating homemade slime become a hit online.

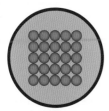

Atoms *(a-TUHMS)*

The tiniest parts of an element that have all the properties of that element.

Chemical Reaction
(KEH-mih-kuhl ree-AK-shuhn)

A chemical change that occurs when two or more substances combine to form a new substance.

Chemistry *(KEH-muh-stree)*

The scientific study of substances, what they are composed of, and how they react with each other.

Matter *(MA-tuhr)*

Something that has weight and takes up space.

Polymers *(PAH-luh-muhrs)*

Compounds that are made up of small, simple molecules linked together in long chains of repeating units.

FACTS FOR NOW

Visit this Scholastic Web site for more information on Slippery Slime: **www.factsfornow.scholastic.com** Enter the keywords **Slippery Slime**

ABOUT THE AUTHOR

Cody Crane is an award-winning writer of nonfiction for children. From a young age, she was set on becoming a scientist. She later discovered that writing about science could be just as fun as the real thing. She lives in Houston, Texas, with her husband and son.

THANKS!

Scholastic Library Publishing wants to especially thank all the children who worked as models in this book for their time and generosity.

Library of Congress Cataloging-in-Publication Data

Names: Crane, Cody, author.
Title: I can make slippery slime / by Cody Crane.
Description: New York, NY : Children's Press, an imprint of Scholastic Inc.,
[2018] | Series: Rookie star makerspace projects | Includes index.
Identifiers: LCCN 2018002685| ISBN 9780531138496 (library binding) |
ISBN 9780531184165 (pbk.)
Subjects: LCSH: Handicraft–Juvenile literature. |
Science–Experiments–Juvenile literature. | Makerspaces–Juvenile literature.
Classification: LCC TT160 .C83225 2018 | DDC 745.59–dc23 LC record available at
https://lccn.loc.gov/2018002685

Design: Judith E. Christ & Anna Tunick Tabachnik
Produced by Spooky Cheetah Press
Content Consultant: Jackie Fego, Certified Teacher. C.V. Starr Intermediate School, Brewster, New York
© 2019 Scholastic Inc.

1 2 3 4 5 6 7 8 9 10 R 28 27 26 25 24 23 22 21 20 19

Scholastic Inc., 557 Broadway, New York, NY 10012.

Photographs ©: 6 graph paper and throughout: somchaij/Shutterstock; 8 bottom background and throughout: Hughstoneian/
Dreamstime; 14 glue: Vicki Beaver/Alamy Images; 20 EM spectrum: Fouad A. Saad/Shutterstock; 20 sun: Panda Vector/Shut-
terstock; 23 top right grass: Ewa Studio/Shutterstock; 24 left bulb: paranut/Shutterstock; 24 center bulb: skodonnell/iStockphoto;
24 right bulb: somchaij/Shutterstock; 24 top: Bessarab/Shutterstock; 25 bottom: junku/Getty Images; 25 top: RGB Ventures/
SuperStock/Alamy Images; 26 top left: PJF Military Collection/Alamy Images; 26 bottom left: R. Koenig/age fotostock; 26 top
right: Laurent Geslin/NPL/Minden Pictures; 26 bottom right: Tony Hamblin/Minden Pictures; 27 left: Kurit afshen/Shutterstock;
27 right: Robbie Shone/Getty Images; 28 bottom: Random House/http://www.seussville.com/Wikipedia; 28 top right: Kevork
Djansezian/Getty Images; 28 top center: Paul Orr/Shutterstock; 29 top left: AF archive/Alamy Images; 29 center left: AF archive/
Alamy Images; 29 top right: jarabee123/Getty Images; 29 bottom left: AF archive/Alamy Images; 29 bottom right phone: Denis
Rozhnovsky/Shutterstock; 29 bottom right screen: Nathan Congleton/NBC/NBCU Photo Bank/Getty Images; 30 bottom: Vicki
Beaver/Alamy Images.

All other images © Bianca Alexis Photography.